Classic Collection

LITTLE WOMEN

LOUISA MAY ALCOTT

Adapted by Ronne Randall • Illustrated by Robert Dunn

QEB Publishing

Playing Pilgrims

"Christmas won't be Christmas without presents," sighed fifteen-year-old Jo March, lying by the fire.

"It's dreadful to be poor," her older sister Meg sighed, "especially with Father so far away."

Mr. March was serving as a chaplain in the American Civil War. The girls' mother, whom they called Marmee, had suggested that with Father giving up so much, perhaps they should make some sacrifices, too. So Jo and Meg, along with their younger sisters Beth and Amy, had agreed to go without presents this year. But soon the girls wondered if they had made the right decision.

"We shouldn't give up everything," Jo declared. "We each have a dollar—we could buy presents for ourselves!"

Beth had a better idea. "I know. Let's buy presents for Marmee instead!"

The others agreed, and soon they were chatting about what their mother would like best. Amid all the cheerful noise, Marmee came home.

"You're all very merry!" she said. "I have something that will make you even happier—a letter from Father!"

The girls gathered around as Marmee read the letter. Father said that he was well, and that he thought of his girls every day. He said that when he came home he would be "prouder than ever of my little women."

The letter made the girls decide all over again to be good and not to complain, so that Father would not be disappointed in them.

Jo woke early on Christmas morning to find a small book called *Pilgrim's Progress* under her pillow—a present from Marmee. Each of her sisters had been given a copy, too. It was the story of someone who journeys through a life of troubles but, by being good and learning from his mistakes, reaches true happiness.

"Marmee wants us to use this as a guide for our own lives," said Meg, and they all agreed that they would. But Marmee was nowhere to be found.

"Some poor creeter come a-beggin' this mornin'," their cook, Hannah, told them. She had lived with the family since Meg was born, and was more a friend than a servant. "Your ma went to see what was needed."

The girls were longing for breakfast, but would not start without Marmee. After an hour, she returned.

"Merry Christmas, Marmee!" the girls cried. "Thank you for our books. We will read them every day!"

"I'm glad you like them," Marmee said. "And now I want to tell you something. Not far away lives a poor family called the Hummels. The mother is sick, and she has a newborn baby and six hungry children. Girls, will you give them your breakfast as a Christmas present?"

The girls' bellies were rumbling, but Jo and Meg quickly began packing pancakes and fresh bread, Amy got muffins and cream, and Beth said she would help carry everything.

A Merry Christmas

"Good angels have come!" cried Mrs. Hummel when the girls arrived at her door. They gave out the food, and Marmee helped Mrs. Hummel with the baby. They left with empty stomachs but full hearts, knowing that they had brought comfort to their neighbors.

At home, after a breakfast of bread and milk, the girls gave Marmee her gifts—slippers, handkerchiefs, and scent. She was delighted with everything. Then they put on a play, which involved many costume changes and lots of laughter. At last, Hannah came in and said it was time for supper.

They thought Marmee might have prepared a little treat for them, but they were amazed to find a huge feast: ice cream—two kinds!—and candy, cake, and fruit.

"Did fairies bring it?" breathed Amy.

"Or Santa Claus?" asked Beth.

"No," laughed Marmee. "It is from Mr. Laurence, the elderly gentleman next door. He found out what you girls did this morning, and he wanted to reward you."

"I'll bet his grandson put him up to it," said Jo. "He looks like a nice fellow, and I think he'd like to talk to us, but he's too shy."

"He seems a fine young gentleman," said Marmee, "so I would be happy for you to get to know him. But now, let's all enjoy our banquet!"

"I wish Father could enjoy it with us," sighed Beth. "I'm afraid he isn't having such a merry Christmas."

After Christmas, Meg and Jo were invited to a
New Year's Eve ball at the home of Meg's friend Sallie
Gardiner. They wore their best dresses, but Jo discovered
that hers had a scorch mark at the back. She tried to fix
it, but she was still worried that it might show.

When they arrived, Meg was whisked away to dance.
Feeling shy, Jo slipped into an alcove by herself. To her
surprise, she found someone else hiding there—a boy!

"Oh!" said Jo. "You're Mr. Laurence's grandson, from
next door."

"Yes," he said, smiling warmly. "Call me Laurie."

They were soon talking like old friends and watching
the dancers from their hiding place.

When Jo began tapping her foot to the music, Laurie
asked her to dance, but Jo felt embarrassed about the
mark on her dress.

"Never mind," said Laurie. "We'll dance down the
hallway, where no one will see us!" And they did a lively
polka, dancing until they were out of breath.

Suddenly Meg appeared, her face twisted with pain.
"I've sprained my ankle!" she cried.

"My grandfather's carriage will be here soon," Laurie
said. "Please let me take you home." The girls accepted
gratefully, and felt very grand as they rode home.

"You know," said Jo later, as they got ready for bed,
"even with my scorched dress and your sprained
ankle, I don't think anyone had a better time than we
did tonight!"

Being Neighborly

There had been a heavy snowfall, and Jo went out to clear a path in the yard. When she looked over at Laurie's house and saw him looking out of an upstairs window, she waved and shouted, "Hello! How are you?"

"Much better, thank you," Laurie said. "I've been stuck inside with a cold all week. It's dull up here on my own! Can you come and visit?"

Jo got permission from Marmee, then hurried over to see her new friend.

They talked about her family, and Laurie told her about his grandfather, who spent most of his time reading. When Jo said that she loved books too, Laurie invited her to look through his grandfather's library.

Jo loved the library, which was filled with books and paintings. One painting was a portrait of Laurie's grandfather, and as Jo studied it, she said, "I used to think he was frightening, but he has such kind eyes."

"Why, thank you," said a voice behind her. To Jo's horror, Laurie's grandfather was standing right there! "So you're not afraid of me, eh?" he said. Then he smiled and put out his hand.

Jo shook his hand and smiled back, and thanked him again for the Christmas feast he had sent. He said that Jo and her sisters were welcome to come and visit any time.

"What will Meg say about this?" thought Jo happily, as she skipped home that afternoon.

Mr. Laurence called on Mrs. March and soon met all the girls—except for Beth, who still found his grumpy manner frightening. Yet she yearned to visit the Laurences' house. She knew they had a grand piano, and she wished she could play it. When Jo told Mr. Laurence about Beth's love of music, he came up with a plan.

On one of his visits, Mr. Laurence began telling Mrs. March about his piano. "No one uses it," he said. "Would one of your girls like to play it sometimes?"

Beth, who had been sewing in a corner of the room, could not keep silent. "I would," she said, "if you're sure it won't disturb you."

"Not at all, my dear," said Mr. Laurence. "I'll be in my study, so you won't bother me at all. Come over and play as much as you like."

So Beth went and played the grand piano nearly every day, and Mr. Laurence began leaving music books out for her. She was so grateful to him that she made him a pair of slippers as a gift.

Mr. Laurence was deeply touched by Beth's gift. In return he sent over a small piano, just for her. It had once belonged to his little granddaughter, who had died.

To her family's astonishment, Beth ran next door to thank him. "I came to say thank you—" she began, then flung her arms around Mr. Laurence and kissed him.

Mr. Laurence's grumpiness vanished. He felt as if his own granddaughter had come back. And Beth was never afraid of him again.

Amy's Humiliation

One day, Amy confessed to Meg that she was badly in debt. "I owe the girls at school at least a dozen pickled limes," she said. "The girls eat them when the teacher's not looking," Amy explained. "If a girl likes you, she'll give you a lime, and you're supposed to give her one back. I've had lots, but I can't return them, because I have no money."

Meg worked as a governess for a family called the Kings, so she had some money to give her sister. The next day, Amy bought twenty-five pickled limes on her way to school. When the other girls found out, they were all especially nice to her—even Jenny Snow, who had called Amy names in the past. Amy hadn't forgotten Jenny's cruelty. She sent her a note saying, "You needn't be so polite. You won't get any limes."

This made Jenny so angry that she told the teacher, Mr. Davis, about Amy's pickled limes. Mr. Davis had banned them, so he called Amy to his desk and slapped her hand. Her face burned with shame.

That afternoon, Amy tearfully told her mother what had happened.

"You broke the rules and deserved to be punished," Marmee said. "However, I don't approve of Mr. Davis's methods, and I intend to find another school for you. Until then, you can study at home with Beth."

Amy was pleased with this. "I wish all the girls would leave," she said, "and spoil that horrid school!"

One Saturday afternoon, Meg and Jo were getting ready to go to the theater with Laurie when Amy wandered into their room.

"Can I come with you?" she asked them. "I've been longing to see *The Seven Castles*."

Both Jo and Meg reminded Amy that she hadn't been invited, but Amy kept pleading. "Oh, do let me come," she begged. "I have nothing to do, and I'm dying for some fun. Please?"

Meg was about to give in when Jo said, "If she goes, I won't! How rude of Amy to poke her nose in!"

Amy began to cry. "You'll be sorry you said that, Jo March!" she wept, and Jo slammed the door as she and Meg went downstairs.

That evening, when Meg and Jo got home, Amy was reading in the parlor and didn't even look up to say hello. Jo ran up to her room and noticed that her notebook— the one in which she wrote all her stories—was missing. She rushed to the parlor.

"Has anyone seen my notebook?" she asked.

"No," said Meg and Beth at once.

"Amy, do you have it?" asked Jo.

"No," said Amy. "I don't have it—because I've thrown it in the fire!"

Jo went pale, then grabbed her sister and shook her. "You wicked, wicked girl!" she cried. "I can never write those stories again! I will never forgive you as long as I live!"

Jo refused to speak a word to Amy. The next day, she decided to cheer herself up by going ice-skating with Laurie. Amy felt sorry for what she had done and wanted to apologize to Jo. So she grabbed her skates and followed her down to the river.

When she saw Amy coming, Jo turned her back. Even when she heard her sister struggling out onto the ice, she thought, "She can take care of herself!"

Laurie skated up to Jo. "The ice in the middle isn't safe," he warned her. "Stay close to the bank."

A strange feeling made Jo turn around—just in time to see Amy crashing through the ice! Jo was horror-stricken, but Laurie flew into action, and they quickly pulled Amy out.

Luckily, she wasn't hurt. Laurie wrapped his coat around her, and they took her home.

When Amy was tucked up in bed, Marmee tended to Jo's hands, which had been scraped by the ice.

"Amy could have drowned," Jo wept, "and it would have been my fault. Will I ever be able to control my terrible temper?"

"Never stop trying," Marmee said tenderly. "I have been trying to control mine for forty years!"

Knowing that her kind, gentle mother had faults like her own made Jo feel better. A little later, she went to see Amy, who held out her arms with a smile that went straight to Jo's heart. They hugged each other, and all was forgiven in an instant.

Meg Goes to Vanity Fair

Winter was over, and spring brought excitement for Meg. She and Sallie Gardiner had been invited to the house of their friend, Annie Moffatt, for a two-week vacation. Her sisters helped Meg pack. They all talked about the fun Meg would have.

"I wish I could take you all with me," sighed Meg.

At first, Meg felt out of place in the Moffatts' big, splendid house. But Annie and her older sisters fussed over her, and affectionately nicknamed her "Daisy." Her days were filled with shopping, outings, trips to the theater, and girlish gossip. Meg soon began envying their stylish clothes and pretty things. Her own simple, well-worn clothes seemed shabby by comparison.

One evening, Meg overheard Mrs. Moffatt talking to a friend about the ball she was organizing for the girls at the end of the vacation.

"I have invited the young Laurence boy for Daisy March," she was saying. "I dare say her mother has plans for them."

"He's rather a catch for her," Mrs. Moffatt's friend said. "After all, his family is very wealthy."

Meg could not believe her ears. How could anyone think that Marmee would be so scheming? Fighting back tears, she pretended she hadn't heard anything at all, and went back to her friends with a smile on her face.

All the girls were looking forward to the ball. It would be a chance to dress up in their finest gowns and jewelry, and to spend an evening dancing with handsome young men.

"I'm wearing my new pink silk dress," Sallie said, the evening before the ball. "What are you wearing, Daisy?"

"Only my old white muslin," replied Meg quietly.

"I have an idea!" said Annie's sister Belle. "You can borrow my sky-blue silk. We'll dress you up like Cinderella, and I'll be your fairy godmother!"

The next day, Meg enjoyed the other girls' attention as they curled her hair and laced her into Belle's low-cut dress and silk boots. They lent her sparkling earrings and a silver necklace and bracelet, and reddened her lips and cheeks with rouge.

Meg couldn't wait for Laurie to see her. But when he did see her, Laurie frowned.

"Don't you like how I look?" Meg asked him.

"No," he replied. "I don't like fuss and feathers. I like the real Meg, the one I've always known."

Suddenly, Meg felt foolish and ashamed. She realized that the other girls had just seen her as a doll to play with, and that she really did not belong in Annie Moffatt's world—or even like it! She begged Laurie not to tell Marmee and her sisters how silly she'd been.

She and Laurie had a good time that evening, but Meg was pleased that the vacation was coming to an end. She was eager to leave "Daisy" far behind.

Experiments

Spring turned to summer, and Beth and Amy had a break from their lessons. Meg's employers went off to the shore, and Jo, who was a helper to their elderly Aunt March, was free, too, while Aunt March stayed with friends. All four girls wanted to have a lazy summer, and begged Marmee for time off from their chores.

"You can try for a week," said Mrs. March. "I think that by Saturday you might change your minds."

For the first few days, the girls had a wonderful time. Jo read until her eyes were sore, Meg stitched new trimmings on all her dresses, Amy drew, and Beth played the piano. But by Friday they were all bored and restless. No one wanted to admit it, but Marmee had been right.

So on Saturday, the girls decided to make a special lunch to surprise Marmee. Jo had never cooked a whole meal before, but she wanted to bake bread and prepare lobster and asparagus, with strawberries for dessert. Her sisters busied themselves with tidying the house.

What a disaster! Jo burned the bread, made a mess of the lobster, and overcooked the asparagus. Then she poured salt instead of sugar over the strawberries.

But instead of crying, Jo saw the funny side of it all and burst out laughing. So did everyone else. Lunch ended in giggles, and promises from the girls to keep busy for the rest of the summer.

"And my special vacation task," announced Jo, "will be to learn to cook!"

Camp Laurence

"Dear Jo, What ho!" the note from Laurie began. It went on to say Laurie had some friends coming from England, and he was planning a picnic for them.

The day of the picnic was perfect. "Welcome to Camp Laurence!" Laurie announced as the girls arrived. It really did look like a camp—there was a big tent on the lawn, to provide shelter from the hot sun.

Laurie proudly introduced his friends—Kate Vaughn was a little older than Meg; her twin brothers, Fred and Frank, were Jo's age. Grace, Kate's little sister, quickly made friends with Beth and Amy. Laurie's tutor, John Brooke, was there as well.

They played croquet on the lawn, then ate a delicious picnic lunch. Afterwards, everyone moved into the tent.

"Ask Kate if she knows any games," Jo said to Laurie. "You should pay her more attention—she's your guest."

"I thought she and Mr. Brooke would pair up," Laurie said, "but he hasn't stopped talking to Meg all day!"

Jo realized that Laurie was right. Meg and Mr. Brooke were off in a corner, deep in conversation— and Mr. Brooke could not take his eyes off Meg.

By the end of the day, everyone was tired but happy. The tent was taken down and the picnic things packed away.

"It's been a lovely day," said Kate to Mr. Brooke.

"I couldn't agree more," said Mr. Brooke, as he watched Meg and her sisters make their way home.

One blustery October afternoon, Laurie, in town for his fencing class, saw Jo go into a building with a dentist's sign over the door. He decided to wait for her. Ten minutes later, Jo came out, looking a little red-faced.

"Was it awful?" Laurie asked.

"Not too bad," Jo replied.

"Did it hurt much?" he asked.

Jo burst out laughing. "I wasn't at the dentist!" she said. "I was at the newspaper office upstairs."

"Why?" asked Laurie, intrigued.

"It's a secret," said Jo mysteriously. "If I tell you, will you promise not to say anything to anyone?"

"Not a word," Laurie assured her. Jo told him that she had left a story with the editor of the weekly newspaper.

"Hurrah!" cried Laurie. "They're sure to publish it, Jo. Your stories are works of genius."

On Saturday morning, Jo grabbed the newspaper before anyone else could see it. She rushed to the parlor.

A few minutes later, her sisters came in. "What are you reading?" asked Meg.

"A story," Jo replied casually. "Shall I read it to you?" Of course, they all said yes.

The girls were enchanted by the story, and when Jo was finished, Beth asked, "Who wrote it?"

Jo couldn't contain herself any longer. "Your sister!" she announced. And, beaming with happiness, she held up the page for everyone to see. "The Rival Painters," it said, "by Miss Josephine March."

A Telegram

November's cold and dreary weather put the girls in a gloomy mood, but they always cheered up when Marmee came home. One afternoon, Laurie was right behind her, which made them even happier.

Before Marmee had even sat down, the doorbell rang. A moment later, Hannah came in with a telegram. As Marmee read the message, her face went pale. While Laurie got her a glass of water, Jo read out the telegram.

Mrs. March—your husband is very ill. Come at once.
S. Hale, Blank Hospital, Washington

The girls began to cry. Marmee gathered them all in a hug. She asked Beth to run next door and ask Mr. Laurence if he could spare some food, as she knew the hospital's supplies would be low. Then she wrote a note for Laurie to take to Aunt March.

"I have to borrow the money for the train fare," she explained, "but I am not too proud to beg if it will help."

Beth came back with a basket of food and wine from Mr. Laurence, and a moment later the doorbell rang. Meg answered, and was surprised to see John Brooke.

"I'm so sorry to hear about your father," he said. "I've come to offer to escort your mother to Washington."

"How kind of you!" Meg said. She invited him in at once and called for Marmee and her sisters. Amid their sadness, the March family found John Brooke's generosity a great comfort.

Preparations for Marmee's journey were under way.

Meg ironed, and Amy and Beth helped Marmee pack. Jo, however, had disappeared right after Laurie left.

Laurie came back with a note and some money from Aunt March. Marmee frowned as she read the note— Aunt March wrote that she had always been against Mr. March joining the army, and they should have listened to her. But she had enclosed enough money for Marmee's train fare.

Suddenly, Jo burst in, clutching a handful of dollar bills for Marmee.

"There's twenty-five dollars here," she said, with a little catch in her voice. "It's my contribution."

"Wherever did you get it?" Marmee asked. In reply, Jo took off her bonnet. Everyone gasped—her long, thick, chestnut hair had been cropped short!

"Your beautiful hair!" cried Meg.

"Oh, Jo, how could you?" wailed Amy, as Beth hugged her sister's cropped head tenderly.

"I was desperate to do something for Father," Jo explained, "and then I walked past a barbershop with tails of hair in the window. They had price tags fixed to them, and that gave me the idea."

Marmee hugged Jo, telling her that she had made a great sacrifice for love. Then everyone got ready for supper and an early bedtime—they knew they would need their strength in the days to come.

Dark Days

The next morning, the girls bravely said good-bye to Mr. Brooke and their mother.

"It seems as if half the house is gone," said Meg sadly. She wanted to stay at home while Marmee was away, to help take care of things. But Amy and Beth insisted they could take care of the housework with Hannah, and that Meg and Jo should go to work as usual.

For a week, all four girls worked hard and waited anxiously for news. John Brooke wrote often, and when he told them their father was doing well, they were all relieved and the mood at home was less tense.

Over the next week, the girls relaxed about their duties as well. Jo caught a cold and stayed at home reading, because Aunt March didn't want to catch it from her. Amy began to spend more time drawing than cleaning and cooking. And Meg spent most of her time at home rereading John Brooke's letters.

Only Beth kept up with her chores, and with visiting the Hummel family as Marmee had been doing.

One day, Beth asked if one of her sisters could visit the Hummels instead, because she had a headache and was very tired. She went upstairs to lie down, and Jo followed her. She found Beth rummaging in Marmee's medicine cupboard, looking red-eyed and feverish.

"What's the matter?" exclaimed Jo.

"The Hummel baby had scarlet fever," Beth replied weakly. "It died in my lap. Now I think I have it, too."

Jo called Hannah, who sent for Dr. Bangs. The doctor said that Beth did indeed have scarlet fever. Amy, who had never had it and was therefore in danger of catching it, was sent to stay with Aunt March until Beth recovered.

In the dark days that followed, Hannah rarely left Beth's bedside, and Dr. Bangs came to see her every day. The girls did not want to tell Marmee about Beth's illness until she was better—but Beth did not get better. Day after day she tossed and turned and burned with fever.

Meg and Jo were overcome with dread—would they have to say good-bye to their precious little sister?

Jo rushed out to send her mother a telegram. When she returned, Laurie arrived. He'd had a letter from Mr. Brooke saying that Mr. March was out of danger. Sadly, they were too worried about Beth to take much comfort.

"I have more news," Laurie said. "I telegraphed your mother yesterday, and asked her to come home. Her train arrives just after midnight."

"Oh, Laurie, how can we ever thank you?" cried Jo, throwing her arms around his neck.

That night, when Jo looked in on Beth, she saw that her flushed face had turned pale, and that she was lying still. Thinking Beth must have died, she roused Hannah, who came running. Hannah put her cheek to Beth's forehead, and relief spread over her face. "The fever's broke!" she said. "Praise be!"

Suffering Aunt March

Though she was away from the worry and strain of Beth's illness, Amy was having a hard time at Aunt March's house. Aunt March was not unkind to her—in fact, she had a soft spot for Amy. But she was determined not to show it, just in case she spoiled her.

Amy felt hemmed in by Aunt March's strict rules and her prim and proper ways. And she had to do chores—washing the teacups, polishing the spoons and the silver teapot, dusting the living room. In the evenings, she had to sit and listen to Aunt March's long, boring stories about her younger days. How Amy missed the warmth and liveliness of her home and family!

The only things that made life bearable for her were visits from Laurie, and the friendship of Aunt March's French maid, Esther. She was kind to Amy and often let her look through Aunt March's jewelry cases.

One day, Esther saw Amy admiring some of Aunt March's rings. "You know," she said, "Madame March plans to give you that little turquoise ring when you go home, if you continue to be a good girl and please her."

The ring was beautiful, and Amy resolved to do all her work without a word of complaint from that moment on. But even the thought of having the turquoise ring did not make Amy happy. As she said her prayers that night, adding an extra prayer for Beth's recovery, she knew that all the lovely rings in the world would mean nothing if she lost her beloved sister.

The first face Beth saw when she awoke from her troubled sleep was that of her loving mother. Meg and Jo could relax, and both slept peacefully for the first time since Beth had become sick.

When the girls woke up, late that afternoon, Marmee finally left Beth's bedside to visit Amy.

Amy was overjoyed to see her mother, and to hear the news about Beth. She told Marmee how she had prayed for Beth's recovery, which made Marmee glad. And she talked about the hardships she had endured.

Marmee noticed the turquoise ring on Amy's finger.

"Aunt March gave it to me today," said Amy. "She told me that I was a credit to her, and that she wished she could keep me always."

"Don't you think you're too young for such a grown-up ring?" Marmee asked.

"Perhaps," said Amy. "But I want to wear it for a special reason. It will always make me think of Beth, who is so kind and unselfish—and being selfish is my worst fault. Wearing the ring will remind me to be unselfish."

"If it will help you do your best," Marmee said, "you may wear your ring." Then she kissed Amy on the forehead and said she had to get back to Beth.

"She is still rather sick," she explained to Amy, "so it isn't safe for you to come home just yet. But you will be home soon."

Amy knew that it would not be soon enough for her.

Aunt March Settles the Question

Later that evening, Marmee and Jo were sitting together. Marmee asked Jo softly, "Do you think Meg is interested in John Brooke?"

"I'm not sure," Jo replied. "But I think Mr. Brooke likes her."

"You're right," said Marmee. "When we were in Washington he told Father and me that he loved Meg and wanted to marry her. He is a fine man, but we think that at seventeen Meg is too young to be engaged."

"Thank goodness," said Jo. "I don't want anyone taking my sister away from me!"

A few days later, Jo found a piece of paper in Meg's desk with 'Mrs. John Brooke' written on it. She had an awful feeling about it.

One afternoon, Meg was reading in the parlor when John Brooke came to the door.

"Come in," Meg said nervously. "I'll get Mother."

"Please stay," said Mr. Brooke. "It's you I've come to see. I hope you're not afraid of me?"

"Of course not," said Meg, blushing fiercely.

"Meg," said Mr. Brooke. "I must let you know what is in my heart. I love you and want us to be together."

"I…I'm too young to think about such things," Meg stammered, pulling away her hand. "I think you had better go and leave me alone."

Heartbroken, John Brooke stood up and walked out—passing Aunt March, who was on her way in.

"What's going on here?" Aunt March demanded, bustling into the room. Seeing Meg's blushing face, she asked, "Has he proposed to you?"

When Meg didn't reply, Aunt March blustered on. "Don't tell me you've accepted him! He's too poor to support himself, much less a wife! If you marry him," she warned, "you won't get a penny of my money!"

Meg's cheeks blazed with anger. How dare Aunt March think that all she cared about was money!

"I shall marry whom I please," she boldly told her aunt, "and you can give your money to anyone you like!"

"Don't be foolish," Aunt March scolded. "If you marry a wealthy man you'll spend your life in comfort. You can do much better than John Brooke."

"I couldn't do better if I waited forever," Meg replied. "John is good and wise and brave and talented, and I'm proud that he loves me."

"Since you won't listen to sense," sniffed Aunt March, "I may as well leave." And she stormed out.

A moment later, John Brooke came back in—he had been just outside the door and had heard everything.

"Thank you for defending me," he said, "and for proving that you do care for me, at least a little."

"I didn't realize how much I care until Aunt March started criticizing you," said Meg.

"We will be happy together, won't we, Meg?" he asked.

She smiled at him. "Yes, John," she said. "We will."

The weeks leading up to Christmas were happy ones for the March family. Beth was getting better, and Mr. March was hoping to be home in January. On Christmas morning, the girls all had gifts to unwrap.

As Beth looked out of the window at the jolly snow maiden Jo and Laurie had built, she said, "I'm so full of happiness! If only Father was here."

Her mother and sisters all felt exactly the same.

Just then, Laurie opened the parlor door and peeked in. "Here's another Christmas present for the March family," he announced. Then he disappeared, and in his place was a tall man wrapped up in an overcoat.

"Father!" cried Beth.

Gleeful cries and loving arms surrounded Mr. March, and he was covered in kisses and joyful tears. Later, Laurie, John Brooke, and Mr. Laurence all joined the March family for a splendid dinner.

"So much has happened this year!" said Jo.

"It's been a good year," said Meg, with a shy glance at John.

"I think it's been a pretty hard one," said Amy, gazing at her turquoise ring.

"I'm glad it's over," said Beth, "because we have Father back."

"And I am so happy to be back," said Father. "Back at home with my loving wife—and my four little women."

About the Author

Louisa May Alcott was born in Pennsylvania in 1832, the second of four daughters. Her family was not wealthy, and so she had to work from an early age as a teacher, governess, domestic helper, and writer.
In her adult life, Louisa became a passionate feminist, and was the first woman to register to vote in Concord, Massachusetts, in a school board election. She modeled the March family in *Little Women* on her own beloved family, and Jo March on herself. Like Jo, she was a free spirit, and loved to learn and speak her mind. Louisa died in Boston on March 6, 1888.

Other titles in the Classic Collection series:

Editor: Lauren Taylor
Designer: Izzy Langridge

Copyright © QEB Publishing, Inc. 2011

First published in the United States in 2011 by
QEB Publishing, Inc.
3 Wrigley, Suite A
Irvine, CA 92618

www.qed-publishing.co.uk

ISBN 978 1 60992 415 7

Printed in China

Library of Congress Cataloging-in-Publication Data

Randall, Ronne.
  Little women / by Louisa May Alcott ; adapted by Ronne Randall.
     p. cm. -- (Classic collection)
  Summary: A simplified retelling of the adventures of the four March sisters living in New England during the time of the Civil War.
  ISBN 978-1-60992-415-7 (PLC - Wibalin)
  [1. Sisters--Fiction. 2. Family life--New England--Fiction. 3. New England--History--19th century--Fiction.] I. Alcott, Louisa May, 1832-1888. Little women. II. Title.
  PZ7.R1584Li 2012
  [Fic]--dc22
                                        2011000339